West Country Bus Memories in Colour
By Paul Roberts

Copyright IRWELL PRESS Ltd.,
ISBN 978-1-906919-19-1
First published in 2011 by Irwell Press Ltd., 59A, High Street, Clophill,
Bedfordshire, MK45 4BE
Printed by Konway Press.

INTRODUCTION

Just over 10% of the UK population inhabits the West Country, but a much larger number will have visited the area, at some time in their life, as a holiday destination. My parents took me to Paignton in 1960 where the Devon General fleet of smart red and cream AECs, with musical sound effects, immediately entranced me. Seven years later a college friendship lead me to pay several visits to Exeter and South Devon, enabling me to capture the local scene when Exeter still had municipal buses and Devon General had yet to be absorbed into the National Bus Company. My employment as a full-time PSV-driver ensured that working visits to the area would follow and soon I was despatched on a holiday tour to Teignmouth and, later in the year, to Newquay in Cornwall. On a trip to Torquay I parked my Midland Red coach in Torwood Street garage where the inspector told me that I must report to him on my rest day and operate a local excursion using my coach. This I was more than happy to do and with a hastily assembled set of notes I managed to locate my passengers at various hotels, find the destinations of Cockington and Totnes and complete the tour to everyone's satisfaction. I can now say that 'I worked for Devon General' even if only for a day – and it nearly got me the sack from Midland Red. I did not realise that I needed permission from my Heath Hayes traffic manager and effectively I had been using the vehicle without the owner's consent!

All the operators included in this book were in the old "Western Traffic Area" as defined by the Traffic Commissioners in the 1960s. This neatly covered the counties of Devon, Cornwall, Somerset, Dorset, Wiltshire and Gloucestershire. I have started the 'journey' in Exeter from where we travel to the south-west. Next we go north-east through to Gloucestershire and finally head east towards Wiltshire.

Photographs taken by myself are not credited but I am indebted to Graeme Coles, Malcolm Keeley and Stuart and Ian Turner for providing slides to fill gaps in my collection, their names being acknowledged as appropriate. I am particularly grateful to Paul Talbot who chose to cycle round the area in 1962, thus providing some rare colour views of the much-missed Silver Star fleet. Thanks also go to

Paul Anderson, Simon Gill, Ian Nicholls, Bernard Slater and Richard Weaver for their assistance in various ways. Finally, thanks again to my wife, Dot, for her support even when it looked as if the project would take over the house.

Paul Roberts
Leicester 2011

Bere Regis & District Motor Services ran a network of stage carriage routes in rural Dorset. Contrary to its name, the company was based in Dorchester where in the late 1970s we find VOR 160, a 1959 Bedford SB1 with Duple 41-seat coachwork. This vehicle was bought from Thorpe of London in 1965 joining a fleet of over 80 coaches, many of which were second-hand. They were kept at several depots throughout the county, at Dorchester, Sherborne, Blandford Forum, Sturminster Newton, Weymouth, Wimborne and, of course, Bere Regis. Photograph Stuart Turner.

Exeter City Transport No.19 (HFJ 146) was the last of a batch of 17 all-Leyland PD2/1s delivered in 1948. In August 1968, this 56-seat bus is temporarily relegated to driver training duties as denoted by the simple addition of an 'L'-plate to the radiator grill. The trainee driver has power to spare as his empty bus climbs out of the Exe Valley up the steeply graded Fore Street towards the city centre. The line of cars ahead of No.19 seems to indicate that the citizens of Exeter have a strong preference for Fords. The Heavitree Brewery name over the bay-windowed shop on the right is a well-known local company that would cease brewing in 1970.

No.68 (XFJ 753) is another Exeter bus, this time a 1959 Guy Arab IV with 57-seat Weymann Orion bodywork, heading out of High Street and into Sidwell Street during the summer of 1968. Further back is a Devon General AEC Regent V about to make a right turn into Paris Street; a street cleaner apparently risks life and limb in the middle of the road as he goes about his trade. The simple brush, shovel and ancient battered barrow is typical of the era. The ABC Cinema, visible to the right of the bus, would serve Exeter for another twenty years before closure and demolition in 1987. More fortunate is the prominent Boots clock, still a convenient meeting point to the present day.

Most Exeter City buses delivered from 1956 to 1966 were fitted with Massey bodies built in Pemberton near Wigan. The Transport Department's double-deckers were all traditional half-cab vehicles with rear open-platforms and relatively low seating capacities. In an era when many operators purchased buses with seventy or more seats Exeter was content to add 57-seaters to its fleet. This near identical pair of Leyland PD2/30s presents a good opportunity to compare front and rear styling of the type. No.87 (87 GFJ), heading down the hill, dates from 1963 and No.82 (482 EFJ) was built in 1962. Many routes in Exeter were jointly operated with Devon General and two of their red and cream buses are just visible lower down the hill. The foothills of Dartmoor form an interesting backdrop to the west of the city.

Exeter City Transport suffered financial problems throughout the post-war period. Finally, on 1 April 1970, all the Exeter Corporation routes and vehicles, along with the Heavitree Road depot, passed to Devon General and the Exeter Joint Services agreement ended. Within a short time, Devon General painted several of its newly acquired Leyland PD2/30s in traditional red and cream. One of these, No.284 (484 EFJ) formerly Exeter No.84, is loading in Paris Street. Route F is a local service and has a street terminus, whereas out of town buses and long distance coaches leave from the main bus station just behind the photographer. Although the bus carries the old livery, its fleetname is in the new National Bus Company corporate style introduced in 1972 and placed just behind the driver's cab. This feature seemed odd at that time when tradition dictated that names and coats of arms should have been placed halfway down the bus. In the distance an early Leyland Atlantean, new to Devon General, is making its way round the intersection with High Street.

Each year from 1961 to 1965, Exeter added five Massey bodied Leyland PD2/30s to its fleet. This policy ensured that they would need to buy a smaller number of buses annually in future years to replace their worn out predecessors. In 1948 seventeen buses had been purchased in one batch, representing almost 25% of the fleet and this became a problem when they all needed replacing at about the same time. When Devon General took over the Corporation buses, it acquired a collection of relatively new, well-presented vehicles that would serve their new owner for several more years. No.290 (AFJ 90B), formerly No.90, is loading in High Street with another of its identical sisters behind. The bus has been repainted in National Bus Company red, direct from its previous Exeter green and already seems to have lost some of its shine in this 1975 scene. The tower block at the end of the street is Debenhams store, originally built by Bobby's of Exeter in 1964 and renamed in 1972. Timothy Whites chemist store to the right was a familiar sight in many towns but following a takeover by Boots in 1968, the name eventually disappeared.

As readers may have noticed on previous pages, Exeter is one of the few places in the UK where bus routes are lettered rather than numbered. This system, which continues in the city to the present day, started in pre-war years during the era of the electric tram. Devon General (DG) No.976 (976 MDV) is heading out of the city on service 'O' on a bright sunny day in August 1968. The bus is one of the first batch of sixteen forward entrance AEC Regent V MD3RVs delivered to the company in 1963 and carrying Metro-Cammell 59-seat bodywork. It also carries an illuminated advert between the decks, a popular feature of the time but one that soon disappeared. Buses destined for Exeter city services prior to this time had open rear platforms in common with those of the City Transport Department. The shopping centre to the right has an identity crisis, displaying signs spelling 'CENTRE' in both the English and American way. Behind the bus is a green Ford Popular 100E optimistically bearing black go-faster stripes – a fashionable embellishment of the period.

This 1965 Park Royal 69-seat AEC Regent V 2D3RA needs all of its left lock to reverse off the bay in Exeter Paris Street bus station during the summer of 1975. Passengers travelling right through to Newton Abbot will be treated to a spectacular coastal journey. Route 2 is still notable today for closely following the estuaries of the Rivers Exe and Teign and using the coast road between Dawlish and Teignmouth. The 1958-built offices of Exeter's local paper, the Express & Echo, are prominent in the background. Following a move by the newspaper to Sowton, on the east side of the city in 1992, the building would eventually become a supermarket.

Peak Hill rises several hundred feet above sea level and lies just to the west of Sidmouth in South Devon. The spectacular views along the coast from the summit justified a local bus service that ran from June to September. The ride saved a long and arduous climb up the steeply graded road from the town. On Sunday 11 August 1968 Devon General No.841 (XTA 841) prepares to depart on an afternoon journey to Salcombe Regis just three miles away on the east side of the River Sid. Such a small bus was quite rare at the time, and this example is a Willowbrook 31-seat Albion Nimbus NS3N dating from 1958. The layout of this unlikely looking bus terminus unfortunately conceals the famous vista, which is behind the photographer.

After the Exeter City fleet was absorbed into Devon General some of the buses could be found in unexpected locations, far from their original home. No.261 (VFJ 996) previously Exeter No.61, a Leyland PD2/40 with Weymann 57-seat body, heads up Dawlish Street in Teignmouth. In later years the manoeuvre would be impossible following the building of a relief road which made this into a one-way street in the opposite direction! In this 1975 view, the only clue to the destination is a paper sticker bearing the legend 'DAWLISH WARREN', barely visible in the nearside passenger window. The bus has travelled from Torquay to Teignmouth on the old coastal route 13, 'the Coastal Special', which had been renumbered 125 just a few weeks earlier. This section is a summer-only extension from Teignmouth to Dawlish Warren.

These Devon General Regent Vs are awaiting departure time in the centre of Teignmouth at the Triangle. No.972 (972 MDV) is a 1963 27ft. 2D3RA with Metro-Cammell 59-seat bodywork, one of the original front-loaders as seen earlier. It is enjoying a well-earned rest having just travelled sixteen miles from Exeter including the long, steep climb out of Dawlish. Behind No.505 (505 RUO) is one of the first of the company's 30ft 2D3RAs and carries a Willowbrook 69-seat body. No.505 is one of eight delivered in 1964 when double-deckers reverted from fleet numbers in the 900s to a series commencing with 501. Its destination display is misleading as the bus is on route 70, not 7_0, and it is not a 'DUPLICATE' but the sole vehicle operating a short local town service.

In 1968 Devon General acquired ten Willowbrook bodied AEC Reliance 6U3ZRs. The first three had more comfortable seats than their sisters, as they were destined to work the Exeter-Torquay Express. In 1974, at the time of this photograph, they had 49 seats but because of restrictive union agreements, they started operating with 41 seats and in their final years ran with 47! No.46 (LUO 46F) is carrying a short-lived reversed livery for the express service which coincidentally is route 46. As the bus negotiates various obstacles in Newton Abbot bus station in June 1975, it is passing an AEC Regent which clearly shows its rear wheel trims, a one-time common feature on Devon General buses.

Courtney Park in Newton Abbot, just opposite the railway station, makes a pleasant backdrop as Devon General No.951 (951 HTT) heads towards Queen Street. Route 116 has brought the bus down the south side of the River Teign via Shaldon and Combeinteignhead. Devon General bought over 120 AEC Reliance buses during the years 1957 to 1970. They had a variety of chassis and engine configurations and bodies by Weymann, Willowbrook and Marshall, this 41-seat version being one of the latter. Additionally many more Reliances went to the subsidiary coach company, Grey Cars, although a lot of these carried coachwork by Harrington of Hove.

No.908 (908 DTT) is one of 23 Roe bodied 75-seat Leyland Atlantean PDR1/1s bought by Devon General in 1960. These followed on from 17 with Metro-Cammell bodies the previous year. From 1961 to 1966 the company reverted to buying AEC Regents, which proved more reliable on some of the hilly routes. No.908 is in Paignton bus station in June 1975, its high seating capacity proving useful on the busy route 12, linking the popular resorts of Torquay and Brixham. In the background is a Park Royal bodied Guy Arab IV, No.256 (UFJ 296) which became something of a 'celebrity' bus. Devon General is the owner but it is in its original City of Exeter livery. It would continue to operate around South Devon in this condition, until withdrawal and preservation in 1980.

In 1967, at the time of this photograph, open-top buses were mainly operating in coastal areas around the south of England. Normal practice had been to permanently de-roof some of the older buses in the fleet and give them a gentle retirement working only during the summer season. Devon General was one of the first companies to buy convertible open-toppers that could earn their living all year round. In 1961, they took delivery of nine such Leyland Atlantean PDR1/1s with Metro-Cammell bodies seating 75 passengers, including 44 on the all-important top deck, where most people choose to travel on a fine day. These buses made a fine sight painted in a special reversed cream and red livery and classed as 'Sea Dogs', each one bearing the name of a historic seafarer. Paignton bus station is the location of No.927 (927 GTA) SIR MARTIN FROBISHER. At the rear, a Western National Bristol K6A No.353 (FTT 704) makes its way to Paignton Zoo on a timetabled journey of 'approximately four minutes'. This bus started life in 1945 as a Strachans bodied utility; it was rebodied in 1955 by ECW, again as a lowbridge 55-seater, and is still preserved in 2011. Photograph Graeme Coles.

In this 1974 view, Gerston Road forms the main access to Paignton bus station, just behind the houses to the right. Future road schemes would eventually turn this major route into a quiet residential cul-de-sac. Another change in vehicle policy saw Devon General obtain nine Bristol VRT/SL6Gs in 1971 and No.547 (VOD 547K) is one of them. These had their 70-seat ECW bodies painted in a slightly modified traditional Devon General livery, the last buses to be delivered in these colours. National Bus influence is already showing in the form of the new corporate style fleetname; within a year, the bus would be painted in poppy-red. At the end of the road is a section of Paignton railway station, used by British Railways Western Region and the Paignton to Dartmouth steam-line, operated, at that time, by the Dart Valley Railway Company.

Brixham bus station in the summer of 1976, DEVON GENERAL proudly displayed over the entrance. In this pre-deregulation era, passengers often seemed to be treated better than they are today. Brixham is a case in point, where the whole bus station complex would be demolished in the 1990s to be replaced with an open square with just a simple bus shelter for intending 'customers' (modern bus companies do not seem to like people being called 'passengers'!). Back to summer 1976, where No.507 (507 RUO) is waiting to make the 55-minute journey to Babbacombe on service 124, renumbered from 12D in May 1975. The bus was converted to open-top ready for this season and is appropriately named PRINCE REGENT, as it is a 30ft AEC Regent V, dating from 1964 and similar to one seen in Teignmouth earlier. Behind is a visiting Bristol VR, thought to be providing reciprocal cover, while a Devon General all-over advert bus is 'on hire' to another operator. Finally, the Atlantean is just arriving from Newton Abbot on the summer only, limited-stop service 190, routed via Marldon, thus avoiding congestion in Torquay.

Newton Abbot was home to a fine new bus station, built early in 1960. As was the trend at that time, the main departure points were laid out in a sawtooth pattern with buses driving in and reversing out of their bays. This gave an opportunity to contrast many varieties of the fabled 'back end of a bus' as in this 1975 selection. There are too many to list individually but on the bays are Leyland Atlanteans, AEC Reliances, an AEC Regent V double-decker and a Bristol RE dual-purpose Plaxton coach. On the forecourt is another Regent V and a Bristol SUL bus. Who would have believed at this time that the whole bus station would be demolished just sixteen years later in order to allow a major office development.

On a glorious day in the summer of 1976 a full load of 49 passengers enjoys a tour along the South Devon coast. The coach, RFJ 824H, is a 1970 Plaxton bodied AEC Reliance 6U3ZR belonging to Greenslades Tours of Exeter, a one-time member of the British Electric Traction group. Rapid changes saw it become part of the National Bus Company in 1971, followed by transfer from Western National to National Travel (South West) Ltd in 1973. As the 1970s progressed, a large number of coaches lost their long-established liveries to make way for the NBC white, with only small red company fleetnames proclaiming the owner's identity. The party is travelling through Dawlish, where sea-views are monopolised by the railway station, just visible to the right. One hopes that the pleasant gardens, laid out in the centre of the town, provide adequate compensation as the group continues its drive along the A379 coast road towards Teignmouth and Torquay.

Plymouth City Transport purchased all its buses from Leyland from 1949 to 1982. No.100 (OCO 500) is the first of the final batch of half-cab PD2s delivered in 1958, completing an order of 90 delivered from 1955 onwards. Their Metro-Cammell bodies seated just 56 passengers at a time when many operators were specifying more than 60 seats in their similar 'Orion' bodies. On 3 August 1973, No.100 has just arrived at Plymouth Bretonside bus station having travelled in from the coastal areas of Wembury Point and Heybrook Bay five miles to the south-east of the city. The route 61 was taken over from Western National in 1959 and consequently is not on the destination blind. The conductor, just visible behind the nearside wing, is carrying a painted destination board bearing the names of the two villages. These are difficult to discern as he is holding it upside down! Photograph Malcolm Keeley.

Plymouth bought a large number of 56-seat rear-entrance double-deckers throughout the 1950s until they amassed 150 such vehicles. The Transport Department was quick to realise the advantages offered by the new generation of rear-engined buses seating no less than 77 passengers. In June 1974, No.179 (YCO 279) is speeding down Royal Parade as the driver gives a cheery wave to the photographer. Apart from detail differences, this bus is representative of 100 Metro-Cammell bodied Leyland Atlantean PDR1/1s delivered in varying sized batches each year from 1960 to 1967, with the exception of 1966. As a rule, to this day, out-of-town bus services run from Bretonside bus station and city services have central timing points on Royal Parade, which is the reason that this location has always been popular with photographers of the City Transport fleet.

Another Plymouth Atlantean is putting on a spurt as it heads along Exeter Road towards its central terminus. This section of the road is on a viaduct running above the passenger waiting area of Bretonside bus station, some 30 feet below. New regulations introduced in 1966 permitted longer double-deckers than had previously been allowed, so from 1968 to 1971 Plymouth bought 33 feet long Leyland Atlantean PDR1/2s. They specified a different body builder, Park Royal. No.254 (MCO 254H) is one of the 1970 batch of buses, others arriving in 1969 and 1971, totalling 58 vehicles. These were the first 2-door buses in the fleet, but they still managed to seat 77, because of their additional length. Another development was the introduction of double-deck 'one-man' operation, also legalised in 1966. As the years progressed, the Transport Department used different shades of red and varied the position of the cream relief. It is interesting to see that the Bedford TK lorry, owned by Rowe & Co, is advertising EAT FRUIT – KEEP FIT, long before the 'five a day' concept had been dreamed of.

Plymouth's vehicle policy took a drastic turn in 1972 when fifteen Leyland Nationals were added to the fleet. These were the first single-deckers since before the war and were set to become the new standard bus. They had dual-doors, were driver-only operated and seated just 46 passengers although theoretically they could add another 24 standing to the payload. In the event just two more batches were purchased, 30 in 1973 and a final 15 in 1974. No.32 (UCO 32L) is just four months old as it loads its passengers on Royal Parade, the main boarding point in the centre of Plymouth, on Tuesday 3 August 1973. The Leyland National works in Workington was keen to spray paint buses in a single livery so the addition of a factory-applied cream roof was an unusual feature. Further down the road, both types of earlier Leyland Atlantean are visible. Photograph Malcolm Keeley.

The final 1974 batch of Leyland Nationals were delivered in all-over red. Possibly the simplified livery made for a lower purchase price and a quicker delivery as it fitted in with the highly mechanised Workington production system. No.75 (WDR 675M) was numerically the last of all 60 of Plymouth's Leyland Nationals and is quite new and shiny as it waits in Royal Parade. Within a short time, No.75, along with its fourteen sisters, would have its window surrounds painted cream, adding another livery variation to the fleet. With 60 Leyland Nationals, Plymouth had the largest municipal fleet of this type, yet they rapidly fell out of favour, some examples being withdrawn after just a few years in service. Leyland Atlanteans would once again be the chosen bus, accounting for all purchases from 1975 to 1981.

Still in Plymouth, two Bristol single-deckers unload at the entrance to Bretonside bus station in April 1975. The front vehicle is No.407 (317 EDV) a 1961 SUL4A. This is a coach version, but the livery indicates that it has been downgraded to a dual-purpose vehicle and converted for 'one-man' operation. It has an ECW body seating 33 and in common with all SULs, is only 7ft 6in wide to negotiate the narrow lanes found in Devon and Cornwall. No.407's one-hour journey has brought it ten miles from the south-east of the city, the outer terminus being the intriguingly named Noss Mayo, beyond the Rivers Plym and Yealm. No.2600 (VDV 769) an ECW 41-seat MW5G dating from 1958, has arrived from the opposite direction. It started from Forder, near Saltash, and travelled from Cornwall via the Saltash suspension bridge. On 4 May 1975, the service number changed from 198 to 73.

This 1975 view of the bus-park at the side of Newquay's Western National garage should be something to make Bristol Lodekka enthusiasts happy. No fewer than six are visible and there are more, hidden out of sight. Most of them are 30ft forward-entrance FLFs, seating around 70 passengers. The four most prominent ones come from different batches. From the right, No.1993 (139 HUO) is a Gardner engined FLF6G from 1962. Alongside is a 1964 version, No.2044 (ATA 125B), an FLF6B powered by the less common Bristol engine. It is in a reversed livery intended for the lengthy limited-stop service 537 from Newquay to St Ives. Next is the odd-man out, a rear entrance LD6G built in 1959, No.1961 (513 BTA). The slightly shy Lodekka is No.2053 (AUO 523B) dating from 1964. A close study of them all reveals a variety of detail differences including radiator grills, destination displays and front window vents.

Once the National Bus Company became established, it started to swap vehicles around for a variety of reasons. Bristol was the main provider of buses to Western National, but in the mid-1970s, Leyland Atlanteans were moved into the area, in some cases to provide double-deckers which could be 'one-man' operated. As well as moving their own Devon General Atlanteans across the border, they were supplemented with such buses from Maidstone & District (21), Western Welsh (5) and, as in this case, Trent (4). No.1003 (RRC 78) has recently transferred from the East Midlands and is parked outside its new home in Tolcarne Road, Newquay in 1976. A primitive ticket machine stand is visible through the windscreen of this 1960-built, Roe bodied 78-seat PDR1/1.

Any bus driver in Cornwall will be expert at hill starts but presumably the learner driver following this Bristol Lodekka would have preferred the bus not to have pulled into this steeply-graded bus stop in Falmouth Road, Truro. It is Wednesday 17 September 1975 and there is a splendid view down to Truro's famous cathedral from this vantage point. Western National Omnibus Company (WNOC) No.2095 (BOD 37C), a 1965 Bristol FLF6B with 68-seat ECW bodywork, is operating the hourly 590 service linking Truro with Falmouth via Penryn. More Lodekkas were added to the WNOC fleet in 1966 and 1967 before the inevitable change to rear-engined buses started in 1969. Photograph Malcolm Keeley.

In the late afternoon of the same day, the 535 service carries a good load out of Falmouth towards Helston in one of the six departures per day offered by this route. Built in 1961 No.2918 (60 GUO) has already led a varied life. This Bristol MW6G with ECW 39-seat bodywork started out as a Royal Blue coach, hence the roof mounted quarter-light windows, and was owned by Southern National Omnibus Company (SNOC) as their No.2255. Next, it transferred to Western National in 1969 along with all its SNOC classmates. A further development saw it converted to a 41-seat dual-purpose vehicle and it is operating in that form in this view. Its final adventurous move, following withdrawal in 1977, would be 970 miles north to a Sullom Voe contractor in the Shetlands, about as far away as is possible to go within the UK. Also heading up Killigrew Street behind it is a 1966 Bristol SUL4A with 36-seat ECW bodywork, No.678 (EDV 533D). Its destination, Penjerrick, is a short-working on the 563 route to Helford Passage. Photograph Malcolm Keeley.

The Moor at Falmouth hosts two contrasting second-hand vehicles on 29 June 1976. 271 HNU, an ECW bodied 43-seat Bristol MW6G, was new to Midland General in 1959. At that time it was No.273 but on moving to Mansfield District in 1969 it became their No.A273. In 1974 it made a final move south where it worked as Western National No.3010 until withdrawal in 1977. Behind is ex-Devon General 'Sea Dog' Leyland Atlantean No.926 (926 GTA) SIR FRANCIS DRAKE, similar to the one seen earlier in Paignton. It has acquired a National Bus Company style of open-top livery and extra safety rails along both sides. It has also been converted for one-man operation and several passengers are queuing up to pay the driver for a trip to Pendennis Point, just beyond the well-known castle. All of the red Devon General fleet changed to Western National ownership on 1 January 1971. No.926 was the first of the 'Sea Dogs' to venture west of the River Tamar where the only visible change is its new fleetname. Photograph Malcolm Keeley.

More action in Falmouth as a three-year old Bristol RE heads through the town at the bottom end of Killigrew Street. Apart from its new-style fleetname it still looks very much a Tilling group bus as this 1972 Bristol RELL6G, with its 53-seat ECW body, is probably too new to be repainted in NBC-green. Unusually for service buses of this period, No.2762 (VOD 105K) is carrying a set of decorative wheel trims. The 567 service is a short cross-town route linking Langton Road, in the north of the town, to the Old Station, near the docks.

Intending passengers at St Ives Malakoff bus station are treated to some of Cornwall's finest views. On 18 September 1975 Western National No.1991 (137 HUO) an ECW 63-seat Bristol FLF6G is loading prior to a journey on the 517 service. This will take it on a ten mile, 37 minute trip from the Atlantic Ocean, visible in the background, to Penzance and the English Channel on the other side of the county. The booking office, to the left, has been recently embellished with the famous 'double-N' logo which rapidly became a familiar sight throughout England and Wales in the early 1970s. This was a result of the National Bus Company's decision in 1972 to promote a 'corporate image' for all of its recently purchased companies. After privatisation in 1986, National Express continued to use the symbol until early this century. Photograph Malcolm Keeley.

The Tilling Group offered its members a rear-engined chassis more than ten years after the Leyland equivalent had come on the market. Once such a chassis was available, Western National became one of the first companies to order the Bristol VR, eventually becoming the operator of the largest fleet of such buses, with 244 of them. This was by a very narrow margin – they had one more than Crosville and ten more than Southdown/Brighton Hove & District! It is April 1975 and No.1076 (BFJ 176L) a 1973 VRT/SL6G with ECW 75-seat bodywork, is on the final approach to Penzance bus station. It has travelled eight miles from St Just, which is on the coast six miles to the north-east of Lands End. Penzance station, the south-western terminus of the old Great Western Railway, is just off-picture to the right which is the reason for the pub in the background being called the 'Railway Hotel'. Photograph Stuart Turner.

More than 2,000 27ft long 60-seat Bristol Lodekkas were built between 1954 and 1961. In 1957, following a change in 'Construction & Use Regulations' six 30ft long versions were built as prototypes, and classified LDL. These were still rear-entrance buses but had an improved seating capacity of 70. No more were built to this specification but Western National owned two of the six and continued to use them for many years to come. One reason for their extended lives was their conversion to open-top in the 1970s and although in more recent years they have changed ownership several times the pair still exist today. On 4 July 1973 one of the duo, No.1936 (VDV 753) is leaving Penzance bus station. The side destination board indicates that its coastal journey will take in Marazion to the east and Newlyn to the west during the 45 minute round trip. The bus is named SIR HUMPHREY DAVY, a famous son of Penzance, whose name was given to the miners' safety lamp. Photograph Malcolm Keeley.

In 1973 Lands End was freely accessible to all. On 4 August of that year, a pair of Western National buses prepares to return passengers to Penzance on the two-hourly service 501. Ten years later the hotel and coastal area would move into private ownership and a contentious admission charge levied. Waiting to leave Britain's most south-westerly terminus is No.1937 (VDV 754) a 1958 Bristol LD6G with 60-seat ECW bodywork. It appears to be a little down at heel in its fifteenth season with the company. The single-decker is a Marshall bodied Bristol LHS6L and although still in the old Tilling green livery, it has an NBC style of fleetname on the roof panels. The 'dormy shed' to the right, with the green painted doors, is one of many maintained by Western National in remote areas. These served as the overnight stabling for buses, which saved costly dead mileage as they were on site to commence service the next day. Photograph Malcolm Keeley.

It is summer 1967 and RJX 250 is travelling out of Penzance along Alverton Street. At the far end of the road is the fine dome on top of the Market House, a familiar feature in the town since 1838. The bus will soon be threading its way through seemingly impossible narrow roads and right-angled bends as it enters Mousehole, a fishing village three miles distant. This 1963 Albion Nimbus NS3AN with Weymann 31-seat bodywork is the largest vehicle that can negotiate the route. Harvey of Mousehole, trading as 'Blue and Cream Bus Service', purchased the vehicle when it was just three years old, after the Halifax Joint Omnibus Committee deemed it unsuitable for their operation. Harvey operated one bus on the joint service to Mousehole at 30 minutes past the hour from Penzance, whereas Western National ran departures at 06, 18, 42, and 54 minutes past and eventually became the sole operator of the service. Photograph Graeme Coles.

Ede of Par, near St Austell, still trades as Roselyn Coaches and, in 1975, had a large fleet of second-hand AECs used for contract work. The bus on the right is a 72-seat Park Royal AEC Bridgemaster 2B3RA, originally owned by City of Oxford Motor Services (COMS). Registered 311 MFC, it was one of ten delivered to COMS in 1961, the first Bridgemasters for the firm. To the left is VKR 476, one of four identical ex-Maidstone & District AEC Regent Vs in the yard on this day in May 1975. This 59-seat AEC Regent V MD3RV also has Park Royal bodywork and carries a traditional style of livery with different shades on body panels and window surrounds. The Bridgemaster is in a new 'stripy' livery, a novel trend at this time.

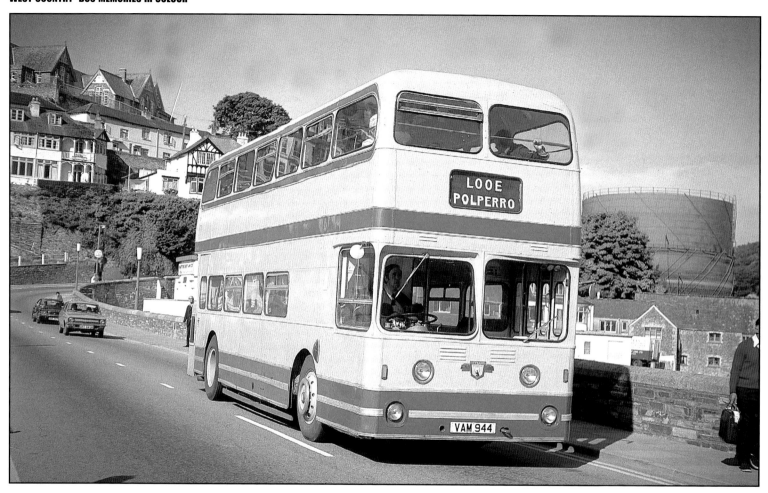

VAM 944 started life in 1960 with Silver Star of Porton Down, a company featured later in this book. Following closure of the firm this bus moved to Wilts and Dorset who promptly sold it, when just three years old, to the Bristol Omnibus Company where it ran as No.7998. After a year it moved to Super of Upminster and eventually to Cornwall, working for Deeble of Upton Cross, north of Liskeard, where its regular duty was on the Looe to Polperro service. On 17 September 1975, this smartly presented Leyland Atlantean PDR1/1 is just completing the five mile, 22 minute, journey from Polperro. It is crossing the bridge, at the top end of the harbour that connects East Looe with the main town of West Looe. Even 35 years ago, when more people relied on public transport, this was one of just ten journeys per day, reducing to six through the off-season period. Photograph Malcolm Keeley.

HOD 877N is a Volvo B58 Duple Dominant 57-seat coach; parked at St. Austell station in the summer of 1975 it makes for an unusual sight. At this time, UK operators were still firmly wedded to the products of British manufacturers, although this was about to change in a then unimaginable way. In the early 1970s Volvo held just 3% of the UK bus and coach market and 60% belonged to Leyland. Over the next three decades, the position reversed until Volvo finally absorbed Leyland in 1990. Trathens, based at Yelverton near Plymouth, took delivery of 14 of these B58s in 1975, representing over 20% of all Volvo PSV registrations in the UK for that year. The Post Office vans awaiting the train represent a bygone era.

In summer 1974, a large private-hire operation from Newquay railway station requires the entire Hubber 'Streamline' fleet of five coaches plus additional vehicles from the Newquay Motor Company. This Harrington Cavalier bodied AEC Reliance 2MU4RA, 569 EFJ, started life with Greenslades of Exeter in 1962. It was destined to become one of life's nomads, wandering around the West Country and taking up residence with a variety of operators. It moved to Webber's of Blisland near Bodmin, Hubber of Newquay in 1974 and finally, in 1979, Silverline of Paignton. It then went on to lead a life in preservation until, sadly, it fell into decline and was scrapped in 2006.

The previous view shows the coaches at the rear of Newquay Station Approach. The rest of the Streamline fleet is parked alongside the development of shops that was built just beyond the buffer-stops in the 1960s, obscuring the old GWR station. Charles Roe of Leeds was best known for building buses rather than coaches, so to find an example of their coachwork carrying a Cornish registration is unusual. This 41-seat Roe 'Dalesman' bodied AEC Reliance 2MU3RA, 485 EAF, spent its life based in Newquay. Purchased new by Hawkey's Tours, it later moved within the town to join the Hubber's Streamline fleet. Just behind it is the unmistakable outline of a Plaxton bodied 6-wheel, twin-steer Bedford VAL and the third in the queue is a Duple Dominant bodied Bedford VAM. In the rear is a Newquay Motors 29-seat Bedford VAS.

This Exeter based ECW 41-seat Bristol MW6G No.2217 (XUO 727) looks to be in fine fettle on a glorious day in summer 1962. The coach is just four years old and would afford a far higher standard of comfort than any of the cars parked on the adjacent spare ground. The Royal Blue name was synonymous with luxury travel to West Country destinations, particularly on routes from London. Its express service network served almost every town and holiday resort west of Hampshire and through to Penzance. At the time of this photograph coaches in Royal Blue colours were actually owned by Western National or, as in this case, Southern National. Photograph Paul Talbot.

In the 1950s and 1960s the name Royal Blue was closely associated with long-distance express services. After formation of the National Bus Company, express services were marketed under the NATIONAL banner. Because of this, Royal Blue coaches were used on a wider variety of operations, including tours, as in this case. On a bright June day in 1974 No.1465 (OTA 637G) takes an afternoon siesta while its passengers explore the delights of Brixham. The ECW body on this RELH6G dating from 1969 looks a little old fashioned but hides a luxurious and spacious interior. Only 45 seats are fitted in a 36ft long body in which many an operator would shoehorn 53 passengers. Sadly, NBC influence had taken over in this view and the mainly blue livery, as seen on the previous page, has been replaced by a bland white treatment. The only relief is a narrow blue identifying band which, in this case, is appropriate to the company name, although the coach is actually owned by Western National!

In the 1960s bus services in Seaton, South Devon, were operated by Southern National Omnibus Company (SNOC). The word 'Southern' in the company's name referred to the old Southern Railway, which had a 50% holding in SNOC from its inception in 1929. A similar arrangement applied to the Great Western Railway and the Western National Omnibus Company, set up at the same time. Throughout the early post-war years, the standard double-decker for both companies was the Bristol K with lowbridge ECW 55-seat bodywork. Two hundred of them were delivered between 1946 and 1950, the majority having Gardner 5-cylinder engines and the rest fitted with AEC or Bristol 6-cylinder power units. In the summer of 1962 No.975 (KUO 988) a K5G is parked, along with a sister vehicle, in Station Road opposite their depot. Following closure of the Seaton branch in March 1966 the road was renamed Harbour Road and from 1970 the old British Railways trackbed would form the basis for the successful Seaton Tramway. Photograph Paul Talbot.

The driver of double-decker No.8320 (UHY 350) will be wrestling to co-ordinate manual steering, a crash gearbox and heavy clutch as he makes the left turn into Baldwin Street in Bristol. Circumstances have resulted in a Bristol-engined Bristol KSW, belonging to the Bristol Omnibus Company, turning from Bristol Bridge and heading towards Bristol city centre! This design of 60-seat ECW bodied bus became a standard for the company with almost 400 distributed around its area. Over 200 were allocated to depots in the city with the rest in towns served by the company in adjacent counties. This is spring 1970 and the Courage Bristol Brewery (formerly Georges) in the background is still working though it would go on to close in 1999. The destination, Filton, was a ready source of passengers; among other projects, Concorde was underway at the huge aircraft factory there.

At a time when the KSW was moving towards extinction in many parts of the country, the author was amazed to find about a hundred of them roaming the streets of Bristol in 1970. The last examples with Bristol Omnibus continued in service for a further six years. Bristol KSW6B, No.8351 (UHY 431) is parked in the area of the Tramways Centre, a title dating back to the time when several tram routes converged at this point. Locals continued to use this name long after the demise of the city's trams in 1941. To the right is the edge of a mock Tudor building, on St Augustine's Parade, which remained as a Bristol Omnibus Company enquiry office for many years because of its prominent position. The telephone box is also worthy of note. It is one of only 50 built to the K4 design and has stamp machines and a letterbox, clearly visible from this angle. For all its apparent advantages, this design was unsuccessful and no more were produced.

In the 1970s many firms bought second-hand buses and used them for staff transport. Licensing of both drivers and vehicles was far less complex before the EEC became involved and providing that fares were not charged this bus would be classed as a 60-seat private car! In the 21st Century, few companies provide such transport and those that do mainly operate small capacity minibuses. In this 1976 scene a well turned out Bristol KSW6B, PHW 966, is carrying a full load of workers from the Brains factory in Kingswood, five miles to the east of Bristol city centre. The rugged reliability of this bus, onetime Bristol Omnibus No.8141, will have made it an attractive purchase for Kraft Foods. Photograph Stuart Turner.

After the war Swindon Corporation Transport favoured a combination of Daimler chassis with Park Royal bodies. In 1947 fifteen single-deckers and ten double-deckers to this specification were purchased, representing approximately one-third of its fleet. Still on the fleet strength in the summer of 1962, five of these buses are to be found at the Corporation garage. There are three double-deckers, of which just one, No.80 (EWV 444) a CVG6 with 56-seat body, can be identified. The single-deck buses both have 35 seats and centre-entrances, an uncommon layout in post-war years. Nine of the single-deckers were CVG5s, which were fitted with Gardner 5-cylinder engines, noted for being prone to vibration and lacking power. The other six were CVD6s with Daimler 6-cylinder engines and these developed a reputation for quiet and smooth running, as well as being more powerful. The photographer has managed to capture an image of the only one of these buses which would eventually be preserved, No.57 (EMW 893), a CVD6. Photograph Paul Talbot.

Daimler was the sole supplier of bus chassis to Swindon Corporation Transport between 1947 and 1961, by which time they accounted for 66 vehicles out of a fleet of 72. Leyland PD2 double-deckers in 1962 and AEC Reliance saloons in 1963 spoilt the chance of a 100% record. No.119 (XHR 119) is one of ten Daimler CVG6s delivered in 1961 and carries a 64-seat Roe body. Although built by the Leeds based firm, it is constructed from Park Royal Bridgemaster parts giving it a tall, box-like appearance. This is further exaggerated due to the bus being only 7ft. 6in. wide. The lower deck carries plenty of passengers as the bus proceeds along Fleming Way in Swindon during August 1974. Photograph Stuart Turner.

Harry's Coaches, based in Cheltenham, was notable for its interesting second-hand double-deckers. He had a phase of buying buses from Jersey Motor Transport, including third-hand London RTLs and this 1949 all-Leyland PD2/1 56-seater. When in Jersey it was No.33 (J 13538) but on transfer to Gloucestershire it had to be re-registered locally. The new registration, DAD 340K, makes it appear (at first glance) 22 years younger than its true age. The other double-decker is a 1959 Leyland PD2/27 with a Metro-Cammell 59-seat body, originally operated by Blackpool Corporation. Unfortunately, the unusual full-front is hidden behind Harry's 'DAD'! Eventually the operation would be absorbed into the Ladvale Group.

A dull day in 1971 does little to enhance the grey and blue of TDF 657, a 1957 Park Royal bodied AEC Regent V MD3RV. Its lowbridge body looks a little care-worn and the concrete bus shelters in Cheltenham's Royal Well bus station do not seem to fit the image of this fine Regency town. The bus is about to make the journey to Gotherington, serving the large housing developments at Bishops Cleeve en route. Although in the livery of Kearsey's of Cheltenham, this company was taken over in 1968 by nearby Marchant's including its stage carriage routes to Alderton, Ford and Winchcombe, all to the north-east of the town. Marchant's Coaches absorbed many operators over the years and runs a smart fleet of buses and coaches to the present day.

Early in 1971 there were just four Bristol KSW6Gs running in the Cheltenham District fleet and by chance, two from different batches are loading at adjacent stands in High Street in the town centre. The pair were originally No.91 and No.92 but following the 1966 renumbering into the Bristol 4-digit system they became No.8562 (UHY 375) and No.8563 (WHW 821). They were new in 1955 and 1956 respectively; No.8562 would eventually be one of only two KSWs painted in the new standard NBC red, surviving for the best part of twenty years before withdrawal in 1975.

The Cheltenham District depot is at St Marks, just north of the town's Lansdowne railway station – the tracks of the Birmingham to Bristol line are visible to the right of the leading bus. The long and narrow drive results in an unusual linear parking arrangement as demonstrated on a Sunday afternoon in 1974. In the 1960s, the depot had an allocation of 34 double-deckers, but soon ten of these would be ousted by single-deckers for the introduction of driver-only operation in the area. Two more single-deckers, including Bristol RELL6L No.1076 (OHU 771F) were bought in 1968; these were single door, seating 53, just seven less than the double-deckers they replaced. The tiny fleetnumber plate is painted in yellow and tangerine, indicating the home depot of the vehicle. Further down the line are a couple of buses in Bristol Omnibus green livery.

Edwards of Lydbrook had its depot at Joy's Green in the heart of the Forest of Dean. A Sunday visit to their premises would be a delight to enthusiasts where, at the top of a series of hairpin bends, they would be confronted with an astonishing variety of buses and coaches. The fleet numbered around 50 vehicles, most of which would be in the yard on this day of rest. A lot of their buses and coaches were second-hand, these AEC Regent Vs illustrating the point during a visit in the spring of 1974. 461 KTG is a 1961 2D3RA semi-automatic example with a Metro-Cammell 70-seat body, while 198 KFC is an MD3RV with manual transmission and East Lancs 58-seat bodywork. The one on the left belonged to the Rhondda Transport Company and the other was originally with City of Oxford Motor Services. This view gives an interesting comparison between highbridge (461 KTG) and lowbridge (198 KFC) bodies. Both buses have the same basic chassis, but having an offside sunken gangway and four-abreast seating upstairs, the bus on the right is about one foot lower than the one on the left.

The Midlands Omnibus Preservation Society ran a tour of Gloucestershire operators on a spring Sunday in 1974. Transport for the day was 76 MME, originally an AEC/Crossley Bridgemaster B3RA demonstrator dating from 1957. After AEC sold it, Barton Transport of Chilwell used it for many years. Next, it had a brief stay with Harry's Coaches in Cheltenham, where it acquired its yellow and white livery before moving down the road to Marchant's Coaches. Here it is visiting Cottrell's of Mitcheldean, where it can be compared with an early 30ft AEC Regent V, SDF 281, an LD2RA which had been displayed at the 1956 Commercial Motor Show. The Bridgemaster is an early example of a low-height bus. When compared with the adjacent Regent the cab and saloon waistrail height is lower, thus giving the entire bus a lower height and avoiding the need for a sunken upstairs gangway. Cottrell's Regent has Park Royal 73-seat bodywork and is fitted with platform doors to enhance passenger comfort on the long journey from the Forest of Dean to Gloucester.

Hutchings & Cornelius (H&C) was an operator based in the Somerset village of South Petherton. They were much appreciated by locals and enthusiasts alike until the sad demise of the company in May 1979. As soon as Bristol/ECW buses became available to the open market, H&C took advantage when they bought an ECW bodied Bristol LH6L in 1972, the first to be sold to a private company. A second similar one, NYD 440L, was purchased in 1973 and features in this line-up. The firm followed this up by adding RYA 700L to their fleet, the first ECW-bodied Bristol VR double-decker bought by an independent. This is a VRT/SL6G with seating for 70 passengers. Also parked in the yard are a couple of coaches. The one on the far left is EMB 967K, a 53-seat Plaxton bodied Ford R226 originally owned by Shearings of Altrincham, and on the right is a coach new to H&C, an AEC Reliance 2MU4RA carrying a 41-seat body built by Harrington of Hove. Photograph Stuart Turner.

There are plenty of pedestrians about in North Street Taunton as H&C TYD 122G cruises along the empty road in the autumn of 1973. This Willowbrook 45-seat bodied AEC Reliance 6MU3R, dating from 1969, has just made a 95-minute journey from its home base of South Petherton. Most of the passengers have alighted in the main shopping area and meanwhile the bus is heading towards Belvedere Road terminus, near the railway station on the north side of the town. MACFISHERIES to the left used to be a familiar sight in many towns. Changing consumer habits saw the demise of the group, which closed all its remaining shops in 1979. Photograph Ian Turner.

Bruton in Somerset was home to bus operator Brutonian from 1972 to 1991, when the Cawlett Group absorbed it. The founder, Chris Knubley, had a vehicle policy based on second-hand heavyweight purchases, which meant that there was plenty of interesting variety in the fleet. No.12 (OVL 495) a Bristol SC4LK with 35-seat ECW body, is parked on Church Bridge, Bruton in May 1978 waiting to make the 16.31 trip to Shaftesbury. Lincolnshire Road Car Company was the original owner of the bus in 1960 where it ran as No.2486. Although one of the smaller buses in the Brutonian fleet, with a Gardner 4-cylinder engine, manual steering and a 5-speed crash gearbox it will not feel like a lightweight to its driver! The Morris Traveller outside the 'Foodstore' helps to maintain the vintage quality of this view. Photograph Stuart Turner.

Brutonian No.11 (771 NJO) proudly proclaims its ownership on the front panel as it leaves Mere in Wiltshire in the spring of 1977. The bus has just completed a reversing manoeuvre in the village, one of three on the route; the others were at Motcombe and Gillingham Station. At the wheel is the renowned Jack Holland, sadly no longer with us. He was the regular driver on the service for many years until Chris Knubley relinquished control of Brutonian in 1986. 771 NJO, a Marshall bodied 53-seat AEC Reliance, was delivered to City of Oxford Motor Services in 1962. It worked for Irvine of Law, in Lanarkshire, before making the long journey south in 1975 to make Somerset its home. Photograph Stuart Turner.

There are no prizes for guessing this location! Yeovil bus station opened in 1968, just a few years before this photograph was taken, acting as a focal point for several independent services. The route from Crewkerne to Yeovil formed the backbone of Safeway Services, South Petherton for the best part of 80 years, starting in 1928. In 1973 the company received a pair of 51-seat Willowbrook bodied Leyland Leopard PSU3B/ 4Rs, both of which went on to give a creditable twenty years of service. This one, PYC 746L, is a dual-purpose vehicle fitted with coach seats, whereas sister bus RYA 646L differed only by having ordinary bus seats. Photograph Stuart Turner.

Shaftesbury & District Motor Services was established in 1976 and 35 years later the company is still operating stage carriage and school services around North Dorset. In the winter of 1977 the depot was to be found at the old Semley station site, hence the goods shed behind the coach. This station was originally built to serve Shaftesbury but it closed in 1966 although railway passengers could still catch trains from nearby Gillingham. Sheffield United Tours (SUT) bought AWA 355B, an AEC Reliance 2U3RA, in 1964 and specified 48 seats in its Plaxton Panorama coachwork rather than the possible 53. This afforded extra legroom for the passengers, a desirable feature as SUT mainly ran long distance journeys including regular continental holiday tours. Shaftesbury and District used the vehicle for a variety of purposes including bus services. The contrasting colours sit well on the bodywork which still has its original brightwork and chrome trim, not always so when coaches move towards the end of their careers. Photograph Stuart Turner.

Much of Silver Star Motor Services' work involved carrying troops on local routes in the Salisbury Plain area and operating long distance weekend leave services. It was therefore quite appropriate that the company was based inside a military establishment at Porton Down, Wiltshire. During August 1962, in spite of the security guards, photographers were allowed to wander round snapping at will. The buses, with their unusual silver and red livery, were smartly maintained and their 'star-motif', mounted in a special front dome moulding, ensured that they were readily identifiable, even after they moved on to other operators. In this splendid line-up, the single-deckers are Harrington dual-purpose 41-seat Leyland Tiger Cub PSUC1/2s. The one on the left, No.33 (RAM 620), dates from 1958, and its slightly older sister vehicle No.31 (PHR 829) was built in 1957. The two Leyland Atlantean PDR1/1s are interesting. On the far right No.35 (TMW 853), a 73-seat bus dating from 1959, was the first of the type to be delivered to a UK independent, while No.40 (XMW 706), delivered in 1961, carries similar Weymann bodywork but is fitted with 61 coach seats. Photograph Paul Talbot.

Pennyfarthing Street in Salisbury was the location of a small yard where some Silver Star buses parked overnight. A corrugated-iron shed and rubble do not reflect the best of Salisbury's scenic attractions but this rare colour picture of No.18 (GWV 360) a 1950 all-Leyland PD2/1, makes this scene well worth including. Again, this standard Leyland product has been modified to suit the operator's high standards. One feature, difficult to pick out from this angle, is the addition of platform doors. These were relatively uncommon on double-deckers from this era, but Silver Star tried to provide higher specification vehicles than its main rival, Wilts & Dorset Motor Services, in order to encourage passenger loyalty. Photograph Paul Talbot.

The last bus delivered to Silver Star, resting safely within the confines of Porton Down camp during an afternoon in August 1962. It is an unusual Trojan-built 13-seat minibus but the familiar moulding on the front dome is still carried on this diminutive machine. For obvious reasons, No.41 (367 BAA) soon became nicknamed 'BAA-BAA' and this name can be seen faintly (and possibly unofficially!) stencilled below the Trojan badge. A few weeks after the date of this photograph, one of the partners in Silver Star Motor Services, Eddie Shergold, died and in June of the following year the company was taken over by rival operator Wilts and Dorset Motor Services (W&D). Many of the vehicles continued in service with W&D, but some, including 'BAA-BAA', moved to the Bristol Omnibus Company. Under its new ownership, it took on the inflated fleet-number of No.2049 and found a regular niche on a special service linking the Assembly Rooms with the Pump Room in Bath. Silver Star may have disappeared almost half a century ago, but enthusiasts still fondly remember it to this day. Photograph Paul Talbot.